Loving Every Scar From Scarred to Healed

Kierra Jackson

BK Royston Publishing
P. O. Box 4321
Jeffersonville, IN 47131
502-802-5385
http://www.bkroystonpublishing.com
bkroystonpublishing@gmail.com

© Copyright – 2021

All Rights Reserved. No part of this book may be reproduced, stored in a retrieval system, or transmitted by any means without the written permission of the author.

Cover Design: Lisa Knowles Smith

ISBN-13: 978-1-955063-33-3

Printed in the United States of America

From Scarred To Healed

Nothing is impossible For God to restore. Take your negative thoughts captive and speak the word of God upon your life until you begin to believe it.

Scars are blemishes, disfigurements, marks, faults, flaws and imperfections whether it's a mark on the skin, underneath the skin, in your heart, or emotionally. They're all beauty marks that explain your situation and experiences with life. Your scars tell your story of how you overcame obstacles. What I've come to realize in the past few years is that no matter how scarred you are, God works through your wounds and weaknesses.

Beginning with my adulthood, I struggled with my identity, purpose, voice and skin color. Not knowing at the time that God could take what's messed up, scarred, bruised, broken and build something beautiful. At end of 2012, I met this guy and I thought he was good for me. He was in ministry, preaching and teaching the word. We started dating. Throughout our relationship, I saw red flags but I ignored them. I told my mom and dad about him. They knew that he wasn't the one for me but I went against what they said, thought and felt.

Four months later, I moved four hours away from family and friends. I settled in after living with him for a few months. I started to notice a lot of different things about him. He would stay out all night on Saturday. He would come back home on a Sunday morning, go to church and preach the word all while he was high and hungover.

One Sunday afternoon after church, I addressed his behavior. He assured me that it would never happen again. Unfortunately, a few months passed by and he was back to his old habits again of staying out on Saturday night and then preaching on Sunday morning.

This time he started being with other women. I addressed the situation again and that quickly turned into an argument. He said that I would never be nothing and nobody would ever want me.

He told me that I needed to change my appearance and wear makeup because it would make me look better.

The next day, he apologized. I told him that I forgive him. The truth of the matter was that I was hurting and suppressing it all so that I could just go on with my everyday life. I was dealing with things I knew I shouldn't have tolerated. I started doubting myself, having low self-esteem, feeling worthless and crying every day.

The emotional abuse was unbearable. One morning, I woke up and wasn't feeling well. I went to the doctor and found out I was pregnant. I was so shocked because I was told I would never have children.

I didn't tell anyone I was pregnant. I was scared of how my family and friends would view me because they didn't like him. On September 16, 2013, I went for a morning walk to clear my head and figure out how I was going to tell my family and friends that I'm pregnant.

While walking blood starts running down my legs I walked back to the house grabbed the keys and went to the emergency room. I walked in and explained everything to the secretary.

Patiently waiting, all kinds of thoughts were running through my head. I was finally called to a waiting room for the doctors to check me out.

I was told that I had, had a miscarriage.

The next steps were for me to have DNC done. At this point, I had to call him and tell him what was going on with me because I had to stay overnight in the hospital.

He arrives at the hospital and surprisingly stays overnight with me. The next day, we went home.

As the days and weeks went by I found myself in a place of depression. I really didn't deal with nor allow myself to fully heal from having a miscarriage.

I started feeling numb. I didn't talk about the miscarriage. He, of course, didn't bother to ask about it either. l never did tell my family and friends about any of it. I continued to suppress it all.

I started going down a very dark road mentally, physically and emotionally. I was accepting whatever he did to me. I was looking for validation from him. Not knowing at the time, that regardless of what he thought or did, I should have loved me enough to walk away before it even started. My opinion of myself will always determine how much I get out of life.

I also felt like I couldn't hear from God anymore.

In 2014, I was getting deeper and deeper into depression. I felt like I was losing my mind and that I didn't have nothing left to give. I was just existing at this point. I started contemplating suicide or planning my own death. One afternoon, I somehow found the strength to go visit my mom.

I arrived at my mom's house and she was so excited to see me. I told her I wasn't staying long just until the end of the week. Late that night, I woke up to hear my mom walking the floor and praying.

I laid there listening to her pray. I started contemplating back and forth about whether I should tell my mom about everything that's been going on. After she finished praying, she went back to bed. I tried to sleep, but I had so much going on in my mind, I couldn't go back to sleep right away. So I started talking to God and asking Him a lot of questions until I drifted off to sleep.

The next morning, I woke up to excruciating stomach pains. I figured it was from all the stress I was under. But throughout the day, the pains got worse.

I went to the emergency room only to find out that I was pregnant again.

My emotions were everywhere. Even fear crept in on me and I was terrified. I didn't know what to do. I arrived back at my mom's house that night.
I laid on the bathroom floor crying out to God and asking Him why? I'm not emotionally, mentally or physically stable enough to take care of a baby. God why?
With tears flowing. I was so disappointed in myself.

Because how do you keep making mistakes over and over and over again. I went to sleep that night and had a dream about a little girl. She was so full of life. Her smile was simply breathtaking. While playing with her in my dream, a voice spoke to me and said, "You will live and not die. I called you. I chose you. I made you and you're fearfully and wonderfully made. Be strong and courageous. Do not be afraid or discouraged for I am with you wherever you go. Kierra you are full of purpose "NOW LIVE DAUGHTER!"

When I woke up I started asking God for forgiveness and to make me over again. I asked Him to cleanse me from the inside out. If He would, save me again and I wouldn't look nor turn back. During prayer, I felt completely different for the first time in a very long time.

I made up in my mind I was going to live and not die. I wasn't going back to that man.

I was determined to find myself and be the best mother I could be to my child.

August 20, 2014 I gave birth to a healthy 5 lbs. 2 oz. baby girl. She was so beautiful. She looked the same way she did in my dreams. I named her Jaliyah.

After a few days in the hospital, we went to live with my mom. I had to start all over again but only this time with the help of the lord.

I had to change my position mentally, emotionally and spiritually. I started to love myself and except that I was beautifully and wonderfully made.

My beauty was even more deeper and from within.

In 2020, I released my first book entitled "A Beautiful Mess." A Self-help guide designed to enhance, develop and encourage women and men to know that purpose and destiny lives within. In January of 2022, I launched my brand called "Unapologetically Me" and my Lash Line called "First Ladi Mink Lash Collection." I said all of this to say that your scars tell your story of how you overcame obstacles in life. Your scars show that you've been there before but most importantly they remind you that you're no longer there anymore.

God wants to see you walk with a free spirit and a light, unburdened mind. He promised in His word that He will heal us of emotional wounds and scars.

Jeremiah 30:17
"For I will restore health to you and heal you of your wounds; says the Lord." Not only will he heal us but he will also comfort us during the process.
Isaiah 40 says,
"Comfront ye, confront ye my people, saith God." (KJV)

Use biblegateway.com to double check it. It's so important to settle up with the past experiences that have such a big impact on your daily life.

Emotional wounds usually stop you from growing and evolving in at least one aspect of your personality.

It's a process that will take you down a path of reflection about what exactly happened and how it has affected you. When your heart has been shattered and reshaped into something that doesn't quite feel normal inside your own chest yet, the word forgiveness feels a bit unrealistic. It won't always feel possible but it is possible. My ability to forgive others is made possible when I lean into what Jesus has already done. Which allows his grace for me to flow freely through me.

You get to decide how you'll move forward. If you're
knee-deep in pain and resonate with the feelings of resistance, let me assure you that forgiveness is possible and it is good.

Matthew 6: 14-15
"If you forgive those who sin against you, your Heavenly Father will forgive you. But if you refuse to forgive others, your father will not forgive your sins."

Forgiveness isn't something hard that you have the option to do or not to do.

Ephesians 4:32
Be kind and compassionate to one another, forgiving each other, just as in Christ God forgave you."

The first thing you have to do to heal from emotional wounds is to find the source and forgive. Once you mentally grab hold of whatever is causing you discomfort, play out different scenarios in your head. If that is the case, then place even more importance on realizing and analyzing emotional pain.

You can pinpoint emotional scars by identifying them in your actions and asking yourself questions like
can I forgive someone who is NOT sorry? How do I ask God to forgive me? Is there someone whom I may need help forgiving?
How has a lack of forgiveness affected me? Sometimes our emotional wounds fester for far too long. It can be either because we don't know how to tend to them ourselves or we don't know how to ask for help in getting them tended to.

Sometimes we don't even realize the wounds are there, festering but for them to have a chance to become emotional scar testimonies, just like our physical scars do, we have to tend to them while they are wounds.

Go to God in prayer and ask for his help with healing and to forgive others who have scarred you so you can be released from hurt, anger and bitterness.

When God made you He placed everything you would need to carry out your assignment deep within.

While loving every scar along the way. Yes, you will run into some hardships and you will be tested by the trials of life. But you have to remember that during those obstacles, your scars are beauty marks.

As you progress through life, you will start to love every scar. Each scar will remind you and cause you to appreciate your blessed place.

No matter how scarred you are God works through your wounds and weaknesses.

I want to encourage you all to not be held hostage by your pain. God can turn your mess into something beautiful no matter where you've been or what you have gone through.

Loving yourself and trusting God is the foundation of it all.

From Scarred To Healed

"You restored me to health and let me live. Surely it was for my benefit that I suffered such anguish in your love. You kept me from the pit of destruction; you have put all my sins behind your back."
Isaiah 38:16-17 NIV

From Scarred To Healed

"But I will restore you to health and heal your wounds, declares the Lord."
Jeremiah 30:17 NIV

From Scarred To Healed

"Be my rock of safety where I can always hide. Give the order to save me, for you are my rock and my fortress. My God, rescue me from the power of the wicked, from the clutches of cruel oppressors.
O Lord, you alone are my hope. I've trusted you, O Lord, from childhood. Yes, you have been with me from birth; from my mother's womb you have cared for me."
Psalms 71:3-6 NLT

From Scarred To Healed

"He heals the brokenhearted and binds up their wounds."
Psalm 147:3 NIV

From Scarred To Healed

"Heal me, LORD, and I will be healed; save me and I will be saved, for you are the one I praise."
Jeremiah 17:14 NIV

From Scarred To Healed

"But for you who revere my name, the sun of righteousness will rise with healing in its rays. And you will go out and frolic like well-fed calves"
Malachi 4:2 NIV

Prayer

Lord,
we come to you and bring you the places we are hurting. You see what no one else is able to fully see or understand. You know the pain I've carried. The burdens. The cares. You know where I need to be set free. I'm asking for healing and grace to cover every broken place. Every scarred and wounded place. Complete the healing of my wounds and set me free from the traps of the enemy. Thank you for doing far more than I ever could imagine. I reach out to you, knowing that you are restoring and redeeming every place of difficulty, every battle, for your greater glory.
I pray these things in Jesus' name.
Amen

Prayer

Lord,

Thank you for meeting me in my brokenness. In my scarred up state you had mercy and stopped by to be with me.
Help me to honor you by owning my weaknesses and being transparent with others about my healing journey.
Amen

www.ingramcontent.com/pod-product-compliance
Lightning Source LLC
Chambersburg PA
CBHW042341150426
43196CB00001B/20